DEAR

WISDOM

BLACK

FOR YOUR JOURNEY TO FATHERHOOD

DADS

WRITTEN BY

JAMAL J. MYRICK, ED.D.

DEAR BLACK DADS: WISDOM FOR YOUR JOURNEY TO FATHERHOOD

To the Black dads who are striving to be their best selves in order to create a new narrative for Black fatherhood and the next generation of strong Black leaders. Don't underestimate your value, King.

To my first-born, K.J., I love you with all of my heart. I hope you experience the fullness of my love, honor, and respect. You're a strong Black woman who has an unconquerable spirit and will continue to set the world ablaze like so many Black women before you... Just like your grandmothers... Just like your great grandmothers... Just like your mother.

PROLOGUE

"Life is a gift, love, open it up / You're a child of destiny / You're the child of my destiny..." Anyone who's followed Jay Z's career since '96 knows the tension he's experienced growing up in life without his father's presence. Society is inundated with messages that Black men do not care for their children nor have a desire to support the mother of their children.

That "70% of Black children are fatherless" rhetoric still continues to be touted on an annual basis when conversations about the Black family come up in the media. In 2013, Don Lemon himself, used the pernicious stat as part of his recommendation to Black people to combat the increase of anti-Blackness and violence after the death of Trayvon Martin. The journalist said, "More than 72% of children in the African-American community are born out of wedlock. That means more than 72% of children in the African-American community are born to absent fathers. And studies show that the lack of a male role model for said children is an express train right to prison, continuing the cycle."

This statement is problematic in many ways, and there's information out now that actually combats this common myth. Lemon boldly claimed that Black children born out of wedlock are fatherless, which is not entirely true because the family structure is varied. There's unmarried couples who have children, but live together, co-parenting couples, stepfathers, and more. Many Black dads are present and engaged in their children's lives.

The Center for Disease Control confirmed in a 2013 report that the majority of Black fathers—2.5 million—actually live with their children versus the 1.7 million who don't. According to many anecdotal accounts, Black fathers are by far the most involved when compared to fathers from other racial and ethnic groups. This same study reported how Black fathers (70%) were most likely to have bathed, dressed, diapered, or helped their children use the toilet every day compared with white (60%) and Hispanic fathers (45%). Brothers, we're out here and we cannot allow others to dictate our narrative! Log in to social media where there's whole Instagram and Facebook accounts dedicated to showing Black dads in a positive, loving light compared to what is seen in mainstream media. There are accounts showing Black dads doing ballet with their daughters and/or kissing the foreheads of their sons. Turn on the television and you might see Miami Heat legend, Dwayne Wade, professing his love for his transgender daughter, Zaya, much to the chagrin of many other Black men. There is a shift happening. Many Black dads are no longer looking to hold in their emotions or be quick to spare the rod and spoil the child.

That's why this book is important. Whether you're a new father like myself or you have a little football team, being a Black dad presents many challenges when told via the eyes of someone living the experience. There's truth and power that's created when we, as Black men, come together to share stories, especially around the topic of fatherhood. And what better way to share learned wisdom than storytelling?! It's an art form that has been ingrained in our bloodlines for generations. Storytelling has been and always will be an essential component in our community: the Black community.*Dear Black Dads: Wisdom for Your Journey to Fatherhood* is not an instruction manual on how to be a parent. There are already plenty of parenting books available on Amazon and Barnes & Noble. Yet, there aren't many books about Black fatherhood on these platforms. In fact, there was a lack with this specific niche. Before my daughter was born, I read books on fatherhood, but I couldn't relate to the information shared. It felt whitewashed. So, I wrote this book to fill in the gap. *Dear Black Dads: Wisdom for Your Journey to Fatherhood* is not the end all be all for Black dads. *Instead*, it's an opportunity for new Black dads to find truth in their own experiences from a raw (perhaps, relatable) perspective. Pastor Rick Warren from Saddleback Church has a saying, *"You've heard that it's wise to learn from experience, but it's wiser to learn from the experience of others"*. That's what this book is: a collection of wise words, photos, and thoughts from Black dads who traversed this road into fatherhood.

Dear Black Dads: Wisdom for Your Journey to Fatherhood highlights the anxieties and learned lessons regarding Black fatherhood from a variety of perspectives. Each chapter, I open with a personal thought/moment and ask questions of the dads about exploring a milestone experience that others could potentially encounter in the beginning of their parenting journey. Some stories will make you laugh. Some stories will make you appreciate your partner more. Some stories will reaffirm your ability to rock fatherhood out of this world. I invite you to also take a look at the photos spread throughout the book. They all tell an added story of the love, care, and joy that these Black dads have for their families.

Black men from different generations, different occupations, and different cultures came together to share insight into the most important role in their lives: fatherhood. Imagine the words in this book as that late-night phone call to your fraternity brother who gives you advice. Maybe you'll see yourself in one of these brothers 'stories. This is community work as we all continue to change the narratives for our children as well as for ourselves. We want to provide better experiences than what our parents were able to provide for us, and as you continue on your road through fatherhood, know that you have a group of brothers cheering you on from afar. I hope that you'll find peace and insight into your parenting journey, no matter where you are on the road. Continue to do the work, brother, and be the man that I know you can be.

CHAPTER 1: IT MEANS I BROKE THE CYCLE

"Congratulations! Do you want to keep it?"

With her pale-skin, brown curly hair, this white woman stole our moment. Both my wife and I were caught off guard by the question.

"Of course!" I proclaimed in my stern, inside voice. A burning sensation came over me and tension in my arms came about. It was anger. Not even five minutes into parenthood, we experienced a slight micro aggression. Now to the untrained eye, it might have seemed like ill-placed feelings; however, I've experienced life on this Earth as a Black body for quite some time. Also, context is important in this instance.

The history of Black bodies and the healthcare system has always been tenuous and is replete with stories of bias, anti-blackness, and more. All one would have to do is go back to 1866 and look up the name Rebecca Lee Crumpler. Dr. Crumpler became the first African-American woman in the United States to earn a medical degree (M.D.), a distinction formerly credited to Rebecca Cole. Dr. Crumpler wrote a book called the *Book of Medical Discourses: In Two Parts* that was addressed to our community and shared our need to take care of ourselves, as she understood that neither the government nor hospitals have our best interests in mind.

The day my wife and I found out we were having a baby, the bias that Dr. Crumpler fought against popped up in my thoughts. We present younger than our actual ages, so our nurse probably thought my wife and I weren't ready for a child. *Is this what we have to anticipate fighting each time we go into the hospital for the next year or so?*, I questioned myself. The constant *Did that really happen?* and *I must be tripping* thoughts were ongoing. But I didn't get too hung up on that because I knew that a much more important experience was happening. I recognized that in a few short months, I would be a father...a dad. I would have to provide for someone who could not immediately give anything back but some goo-goos and ga-gas.

Fatherhood is important, but what does it mean to be a Black father? A Black man who is charged with raising their children to be the best version of themselves is powerful beyond belief. What does this mean during this generation of Black dads?

What does being a black father mean to you?

"...it means everything to me. I have the task of furthering our lineage/culture in a new way. That is a heavy load but also a pleasure to carry." – O. Nwaneri

"It's a true blessing. To truly be able to mold a young life is truly a God send. As black fathers, we must make sure we bring our children up in the right way." –R. Smith

"...being a positive influence in the lives of my daughters and showing them how a man should treat a woman. Being a positive male influence in their lives and giving them [my girls] all the love and care they deserve." –J. Spears

"...I'm representing for all of the great active fathers out in the world. The media portrays a different image at times, but I personally know a lot of great Black fathers." – O. Alebiosu

"Being the architect of possibilities for my family. A first-class opportunity to defy the odds and create a legacy that builds on the history of our family to make every generation connected to us better." –Dr. Yuille

"...being a creator to build nations..." –X. Postell

"...it means everything to me. It's my inspiration, my reason, and my greatest blessing." –T. Davis

"...everything, but I cannot confidently say that I entered fatherhood with the conscious mindset of being a Black father but rather a great father. My son is only one year and nine months of age, but from his birth, I understood the importance of role modeling for him—demonstrating what it means to love and be loved...demonstrating how a family should work together to tackle everything from hard times to chores. I entered my [parenting] journey understanding that my son needs to see me there every morning changing his diapers, feeding him, playing with him, reading to him, making eye contact, loving his mother, and much more. I understood that his unconsciousness had to be my deepest and utmost consciousness, as anything else was unacceptable. I understood that I was shaping a human—a Black man. So, being a Black father means everything because I understand the importance of my role in building a Black man who will influence a family that will shape the culture and ultimately change lives." –Dr. Gordon

"I have the blessing to leave a legacy. My goal is to raise a child to be great in many facets [of life] and be a change agent in the next generation."-A. Obasohan

CHAPTER II: I AM A PART OF CREATING A BETTER FUTURE FOR THE BLACK WORLD.

As a new Black father, I often reflect on my own journey in life, especially my relationship with my parents. One of the things I appreciated about my mother, was that she ensured I understood what this skin of mine meant. She made sure I knew that being Black was not going to be easy, but I can/will weather the storm. Not in an "open your third-eye, burning sage and incense" type of way, but more of an "affirmation in spite of what the media shares" type of way. These lessons came in the form of whoopings, the "glare", and of course, the "conversation". My mother taught me these lessons to build me up as a Black man who understood that the world is/was against me while not being afraid of bravery in the face of whiteness and white people. But how can I do this in a healthy way that doesn't require trauma? How can I educate my own child about their Blackness in a world void of pain? Physical and emotional abuse is oft attributed to parenting of Black children, but I often wonder how can I educate my child about her Blackness without harm?

How do you incorporate blackness into your parenting style?

"...Black art, movies, books...all Black everything! The school system will try to make Black children believe they are less than or inferior. You, as their father, must counter act that reality." –Dr. Yuille

"...preach history because you have to know where you come from." –A. Obasohan

"...I am not really a conscious Black person in the sense of Black or African-American identity being at the forefront of my mind. I understand that I am Black, and I understand the implications of being Black in America. I also know that it is important to show up as a Black person, such as wearing my natural hair, supporting Black artists, and acknowledging my people. However, I cannot say that I have made any effort to incorporate Blackness into my parenting style—unless you include buying books with representation so he [my son] can see people who look like him in his literature. Thematically, I hope that my son sees what it means to be a strong Black family through our everyday actions." – Dr. Gordon

"...they may receive 'pops' which many people equate to slave mentality. We celebrate Juneteenth. We eat our cultural Caribbean and soul food. We purchase products that represent us from books to clothing. My daughters have natural hair, and we use natural products on our body. We listen to the hip hop, neo soul, R&B, and some of this new age trap music." –R. Beasley

"...by being an example of healthy Black love. Purposefully celebrating and honoring our culture, tradition, and holidays. By giving our child a 'Black name' so that she can always identify as a Black person moving in this world." –T. Davis

"...I honestly try to instill three values given to me by my Nigerian parents: family values, respect, and hard work. My wife and I make sure to emphasize these values. This society wasn't built for us, so making my child understand self-worth is important." –O. Nwaneri

"...teaching strength, wisdom, and just breaking the 'Black father not being there' cycle." –R. Bottoms

"...by showing them that we are the underdogs while teaching them that if we fail, it is no one's fault but our own. We can neither blame other ethnicities for us [Black people] not making it in life nor put anyone down because they look or act differently than we do." –J. Spears

"...music. A lot of the music that I loved growing up, I try to have my son listen to. I lean more toward stories and/or music that are rich in Blackness when picking what my child should and should not watch or listen to." –R. Smith

CHAPTER III: LOVE YOUR KIDS NO MATTER WHAT THEY DO.

An old piece of wisdom I remember from years ago is look to the past to inform your present and prepare for the future. This advice has stuck with me ever since. When I'm having a difficult time, I think about the prior hardships I've had in my lifetime to push me through and to the next level. When I forget who I am, I immediately remind myself by reflecting on my past.

Sometimes, the best advice comes from those who've traversed this path ages before us. As Black men, we hold a wealth of knowledge that's been passed down from generations. As Black fathers, we have to take heed to this wisdom to ensure we're creating a better future for own children.

What's the best advice you received about fatherhood?

"...don't take the first few months personal, especially if the mother is breastfeeding. There's absolutely nothing that comes between a newborn child and their mother.

The bond that you will share will come months later." –R. Prescott

"...love your kids no matter what they do. Help them find their passion and teach them how to reach their goals." –J. Kirk

"...I never received advice. My father—and other father figures in my life —lead by example. They supported their child(ren) even if they didn't always understand their child(ren)'s decisions or thought processes. As for me, they acknowledged my feelings and gave me positive feedback that was essential in my growth from a boy to a man. Most importantly, my father and father figures showed me that they were imperfect humans. From their experiences, I've learned that you'll never be ready to be a father but you must be willing...everything else will fall into place." –D. Shannon

"...I've received great wisdom about fatherhood, but the one piece of advice that stands out the most is not being afraid to tell your child(ren) when you're wrong. Never be ashamed to say, 'Son/daughter, I was wrong and this is how I'm going to make it right.' We, as parents, don't know everything. And since we're imperfect, our children will see our imperfections. This is nothing to be ashamed of but something to embrace to let your children know you're striving for perfection. This will also strengthen your relationship with them." –A. Arbyummi

"...being a father means stepping outside of yourself to see yourself as your child does. That will help you understand what they need the most. There is no manual for fatherhood because children are as unique as your fingerprints." –C. Boldon

"...take advantage of every moment. As a father, you get a chance to mold a leader (son) of a future family and an opportunity to show a little girl how she is supposed to be treated." –J. Martin

"...self-care is important. Of course, you'll both [you and your partner] want to be super parents, especially with your first child. However, each of you need to take time for yourself to reset. 'Parent 'is the best title you'll ever have, but it's not the only one." –R. Irving

"...stay around! Get as many pictures as you can with your kids and family. Work it out with the mother, no matter the cost." –A. Bratton

"...never bring work home to the children. They deserve to be greeted by dad...not the attitude from the outside world that you deal with on a daily basis." S. Douglas

"...you cannot raise your children based on how someone else raises theirs. You are not them nor are your children theirs. You can follow what they say in theory, but every situation is different and methods must be tweaked to suit your family situation."
-J. Spears

"...it's a marathon not a race. There will be tough days, and there will be easy days. The key is to always show love to your child letting them know you will always be there for them." –R. Smith

"...your child is not yours. Yes, you are their parent, but they are their own entity. They are not an extension of your failed ambition, etc. They have a life they must live out, and this will continue long after you're gone. As a parent, your job is to guide your child as they grow, equip them with the best tools, and step aside when the time is right. It's not your job to live their whole life for them...just be a great guide. #trainingwheels" –O. Nwaneri

"...provide daily words of affirmation and empower them to be happy with themselves in order to be happy with others. I let my daughter know that she's an intelligent, beautiful Afro Latina." –O. Alebiosu

"...your job as a father is not to raise another you but to support and help your child find who they will become in life." –T. Davis

"...being present is the best gift. So, be with your spouse and child(ren). Never give up on them. Show them what you believe, and live it out every day."
–J. Mason

"...it is a lifelong responsibility." –Dr. Yuille

"...winners find a way to win. Losers find excuses." –N. Richardson

Chapter IV: Don't over think. Just be present.

I imagine the first six months of being a father to be tiresome, anxiety-ridden, and scary. I've heard people say that they struggled leaving the hospital because it was all on the parents to ensure that the baby is healthy and alive from that point on. One of my biggest concerns as a first-time dad was trying to balance it all. For years, there's been a sense of freedom to come and go as my wife and I pleased. We didn't have to worry about securing a babysitter or taking time out of our day to make sure that someone else was fed.

Between my career, fraternity, friends, and marriage (among other obligations and interests), I wondered how I would manage it all. How do parents find the time to manage it all?! Of course, many of the Black dads who participated in this book wanted to share some insight into the first 30, 60, 90, and 180 days postpartum and give advice on how to navigate this new life transition.

What advice will you give for the first 30-days postpartum?

"...try to establish a routine that allows you to have some time for yourself AND your spouse. Create a nap schedule and a bedtime routine, and don't deviate from it. First-time parents [typically] make it all about their new addition and quickly lose sight of everything else. Also, be mindful that everyone is learning, adapting, and exhausted. The woman's body goes through so much, and we will never understand that. So, be patient, be encouraging, and validate your children's mother. Compliment her as often as possible." –R. Prescott

"...keep the baby up during the day as long as you can so they sleep most of the night! Make sure you're hands-on helping with the baby, especially while wifey is recovering herself. If you don't want your baby sleeping in your bed at five years old, put them in their own bed and room early. Don't start nothing you ain't willing to keep up!" –J. Kirk

"...enjoy it, relax, and take the time to fall in love with your child. They'll stop looking so strange soon. Also, get involved. Feed them skin-on-skin, talk to them, sing to them, and rap to your child. Pour into them. Remember, you and your child don't have to be perfect. Forgive yourself for whatever mistakes you've made and teach from them and your successes. Start your daily affirmation with your child now. Hold them up in the mirror every day, and pour positivity into them." –K. Burrell

"...as I mentioned earlier, be a willing father. Change the narrative. There are no gender roles when it comes to being a father in my house. I pride myself in being able to provide for my children in every aspect. Change those diapers, get up in the middle of the night to give them that bottle, and rock them to sleep. Cherish those moments. They are fleeting."
–D. Shannon

"...don't panic, but help your wife as much as possible— help make it easier for her. It will turn out great for the child."- A. Arbyummi

"...the first 30 days as a father were very scary to me, but

I never let my wife or son see it. I would tell a new dad to enjoy the moment and appreciate the newness of fatherhood. Be patient with your child's mother, and give them the help they need to nurture your newborn together." – J. Martin

"...be patient with your spouse. Pregnancy is traumatic as hell, and in some cases, a near-death experience. Therefore, give her a break as much as possible. She'll want to do everything the majority of the time, so when she wants a break, jump at the chance." –R. Irving

"...have a cigar with the boys. Take FMLA (you have a year to do it). Enjoy your time with your kids. Take lots of pictures, and enjoy every minute. As tired as you may be, help out! Mom will love you for it, even though she will act like she's all by herself. Be there!"
–A. Bratton

"...there will be a lot of sleepless nights. There will be days where you'll think to yourself, *Damn, my life will never be the same.* Keep the faith. It gets better as time goes on." – R. Smith

"...forget about sleep. LOL. Pay attention to the needs of Baby and most importantly, Mommy. Postpartum depression is real, and men usually quickly dismiss it." –O. Alebiosu

"...DO NOT TURN DOWN ANY HELP! Also, the first 30 days is going to be a challenge. Don't take anything personal from your queen. Be over-attentive to you wife, a big component of being the best father you can be is also being the best husband/spouse/partner you can be." –T. Davis

"Support your wife or child's mother. The mother of your baby will need your help weather or not she explicitly asks. If this is your first child, then this is new territory, which can be scary and lonely. Therefore, it's necessary to have support at every juncture. Sure, your wife might be able to breastfeed and might not need you there between 2:00 A.M. and 4:00 A.M. when she is feeding the baby, but you need to be there. You need to support her, check if she needs anything, and provide companionship. Honestly, you need to get to know your child; however, mother support is critical. Imagine your body not belonging to you, feeling like you are only used to provide, and being taken from 24 hours a day without anyone there to support you—lonely, right?"- Dr. Gordon

"...spoil your spouse. Support them. Be there to fortify the choice you made. Decide in advance that if you're going to lay there, you will stay there. It carries over to a sign of dependability and confidence with your children." –J. Mason

What advice will you give for the first 60- days postpartum?

"...still practice patience because your child will cry. And cry. And cry. And cry some more. You could've fed your child and changed their diaper and they will still cry. It's a beautiful ride overall, but sometimes the urge to yell will happen." –R. Irving

"...the first 60 days are tough. You will lose sleep, and the baby will not stop crying, and most importantly, you still won't know what you're doing. Find some consistency in what you do on a daily basis, and then talk to your child every moment you get so they understand the commands in your voice." –J. Martin

"...mom is tired. Give her a break. Don't buy that baby Jordans!" –J. Wimbley

"...don't start nothing you ain't willing to keep up...this includes pacifiers. Get rid of pacifiers early if you don't want them [kids] with it for a long time. But if you let them keep it, put a bunch in their bed so they can find it themselves in the middle of the night." –J. Kirk

"...take a picture once a month for a year. Create a folder and add the images to the folder monthly. After month 12, revisit all 12 images. It'll be a super cute experience." –R. Prescott

"...how you speak to your spouse will be the tone your children see as acceptable to receive communication. Your relationship with your spouse overflows to them. Sixty days is short but can feel like a mini lifetime with a hands-on experience. Don't miss a day." –J. Mason

What advice will you give for the first 90- days postpartum?

"...at this point, you should be a pro at the little stuff like diapers, bath time, changing clothes, and nap time. Seems like there isn't time for yourself, or better yet, time to get freaky with your wife. It will get better. Just hang on." –K. Bryant

"...you're gonna make mistakes. It's okay." –O. Nwaneri

"...learn to balance the time between being a dad and

being yourself." –S. Douglas

"...you're still learning yourself, your child, and your spouse. Be patient with yourself when you yell or lose it. Communicating at all times will help both mom and dad."- A. Bratton

What advice will you give for the first 180- days postpartum?

"...encourage one another to have some time away from the family...social time, not errands or work. Sharing responsibilities also help. I mentioned a schedule for the newborn, around the six-month mark I would recommend a traditional or non-traditional routine or list of responsibilities for spouses. Find a group of fathers and establish some play dates. Invest in a good stroller and take the little on a walk/run a few times a week." –R. Prescott

"...pat yourself on the back. At six months, you have pretty much laid the groundwork for how you're going to be as a father. The circumstances will change, of course, but the way you show that you love and support them won't." –D. Shannon

"...lay on the ground with them at floor time and mimic their movements. Allow them to see themselves in you." – C. Boldon

"...your child is six months now. You are proud of who you are as a father by now. You'll want to show and talk to others the things your kid can do. At this age, my advice is to read to them and take more responsibility from the mother by giving her a break. My son is blessed to have two parents in the house, and I want him to see the teamwork it takes to raise one little kid." –J. Martin

"...at six months, mine were starting to crawl and were getting into stuff, and I had to clean up even more than usual. Stick with the feeding, nap time, and bedtime routines, even on the weekends. Try not to let chores pile up. Take the baby to the park. Go out for walks. Sing those nursery songs (e.g., ABCs and 123s). Know that it's never too early to start the educational process." –J. White

"...strap in, and enjoy the ride. This is only the beginning. Allow your child to be a child and explore and grow. Try not to stress yourself out too much." –K. Burrell

"...focus on your real estate, and look up how to pay off your home in seven to ten years. Use these plans to cut down interest. Have fun because the little one will only be little for so long." –A. Bratton

"...keep your baby comfortable and listen to when and why they cry because they will let you know what they need or want. By this time, they respond to stimulus very well. They will let you know what's going on if you are patient and attentive." –J. Spears

"...it's always important to support your child's mother and make sure she's in a good place. Beyond that, I would encourage all fathers to lean into the experience. Feed your child, read to them, sing to them, dance with them, be silly together, but most importantly, be intentional about everything. The older your child becomes, the more observant they will be. They are always watching, listening, and learning, so be sure to manage your emotions, your expressions, and your behavior toward your child's mother." –Dr. Gordon

CHAPTER V: POTTY TRAINING WILL MAKE A MAN OUT OF YOU.

When I first found out that I was going to be a father, I immediately thought about all of the cool things that I would do with my child that I was not always privy to: trips to Disneyland, international travel, and maybe even a wrestling show or two. I thought about the matching sets of clothes we'd wear out to stunt on everybody and their gran-gran. I also thought about the moments in between that I shouldn't overlook...the first smile or the speedy growth. I've seen some of my closest friends 'kids literally grow up in a matter of months, and I saw the love and joy of the parents blossom with each passing day.

Everyone hears about the difficult parts of parenthood (i.e., the wiping of diapers, the sleepless nights, the constant crying, etc.). It's a role that many of us will only understand when the role is bestowed upon us. But what about the good moments? What are some of the experiences of Black fatherhood that you leave you in awe? As humans, I think we tend to lean toward the negative because it's easy to notice when things are bad as opposed to when things are good. It's important that we have a wide perspective of what being a Black dad means. Knowingly, this book includes the positive stories as well as the others. Some of these dope Black dads could not wait to share some of their favorite moments with their children.

****

"When my daughter was two years old, she tried to squeeze past her mother but couldn't fit. She took a few steps back and said politely, "Excuse me, nigga." One of funniest moments to date. My daughter said she learned that word from her great grandma." –R. Prescott

"Being in the delivery room when my son was born and our doctor letting me actually pull my son out!" –J. Kirk

"As we travel through this parenting journey, Whitley and I expected to encounter some road blocks, adjustment pains, and parenting fails. Well, I am pleased, humored, and embarrassed to tell you about our biggest fail yet with two words: aloe vera.

So, unfortunately Caleb was diagnosed with a small bit of baby eczema. (To the expecting first-time parents, this is very common.) Whit and I—being first-time parents— bought everything on the baby aisle that read unscented, fragrance-free, and eczema-relief. However, we were given another suggestion by family and elders to go a more nat- ural route and rub aloe vera straight from the plant on him.

Whitley brought home from the store what was easily the largest jug of aloe vera I've ever seen. I've learned to stop asking questions, so I didn't ask any. Apparently the closest Walmart, which wasn't a good choice but conveni- ent, didn't have any aloe vera plants...or so she said. So, I stopped gawking at this one gallon, Costco-bulk-size bot- tle of aloe vera enough to prep Caleb for application. I poured a bit in a cup and grabbed a towel and headed over to Whitley as she held him. I slathered him in it. I mean, we bathed him in it—the gel was all over his body. There was not one external part of my son that wasn't covered in aloe vera.

Afterward, Whitley handed him to me and I put his clothes back on. We proceeded with our evening ritual of watching Jeopardy. Twenty minutes later, Whit opened the refrigerator and something caught her eye on the bottle which read "Drink to your health." She continued to read and calmly called my name in the tone that made me think I was in trouble. I answered as I looked down to make sure my son was alive and okay, and then I looked up. She had the look of dire concern. "Babe, this is juice." I had to be supportive so I couldn't laugh hysterically like I wanted to. I quickly took off my son's clothes off so he could get a nice long bath...then, I laughed hysterically." –C. Boldon

"My favorite story thus far is the one of my son's birth. His due date was supposed to be November 3rd, but there was an emergency delivery and he came on September 17th. I was shown very early that my son is a fighter, he marches to the beat of his own drum, and he is stubborn. – R. Irving

"I was always one for gadgets and high-end gifts, but kids are simple. Mine like to go camping and take road trips., and I love it. I almost hate that they have to grow up at times. I spent big money trying to get all the cool toys, and when it came down to it, the kids loved the little dollar store toys that we used to play with growing up. This showed me that my kids enjoyed the little things. I even bought Nintendo games and they enjoyed them as I did growing up. That said, my advice is to relive your childhood through your parent eyes. Be there, no matter how much you mess up...your kids don't know. Be a dad!" –A. Bratton

"It's not a long story, but it's still my favorite moment. I couldn't get my daughter to sleep in her crib during the first two weeks of being home, and one night, she struggled for a good hour to remain sleep. That night, I slept on the hardwood floor next to her crib, and it was then that I realized how important my presence was/is to my child. A two-week-old infant was able to settle and rest just because her dad was near her. That was the greatest moment of being a father for me." –S. Douglas

"Dads who have tea parties with their daughters regardless of how masculine of a man they are...to me, doing things like that means they are willing to go above and beyond the call of duty to make their little girls happy." –J. Spears

"This is not really a long story, but more like a moment. Every night, we [my partner and I] alternated between who put my daughter to bed. Months went by, and I honestly don't realize how fast my child was progressing; but one night, it hit me. I read the bedtime story and said goodnight. Then, for the first time, I heard, 'Dad, you're the best.' That's all I needed to ever hear #prouddadmoment " –O. Nwaneri

"I love sharing moments with my daughter like singing our favorite songs in the car to the playlist we've created. We truly are a dynamic duo, and she's a daddy's girl." –O. Alebiosu

"I don't know, as I feel like every day is a memory. Jamal, I love my son so much. I think about him and I want to cry. I love watching him learn. I love his facial expressions. I love watching him process things. I love the way he looks at me and how much he loves me. I love how he smiles when I hold him and when my wife and I both wrap our arms around him and kiss him. Everything is my favorite... even the hard times." –Dr. Gordon

"My favorite story would be in the form of moments. I love when I go to the store or run a few errands and come back home to my 'lil man' smiling and fighting to get out his mother's arm to get to me! Aaah, that feeling doesn't ever get old!" –A. Arbyummi

"My favorite story about fatherhood is the moment I thought I had my girls figured out only to find out I had (and still have) no clue. With that being said, I'd have to say it's less of story and more of movie with no ending. Stay ready so you don't have to get ready. They sure will. LOL." –D. Shannon

"One evening, I cranked my car up before work and as I went back out to leave, my son was sitting in the back seat because he didn't want me to leave." –R. Bottoms

CHAPTER VI: FATHERHOOD IS THE BEST HOOD.

Attending therapy for the past four years helped me immensely. Sitting in that chair for an hour on a monthly basis unpacking my own toxicity, pains, and hurts was a struggle at first. I'm not perfect, but I'm much better than I was. It's something about letting the burdens of the world that rest on your shoulder fall to the wayside through healing and conversation. Not only has therapy challenged me to improve in all aspects of my life, it has also pushed me to confront previous trauma that hindered me for ages. The biggest boulder was reconciling my relationship with my own father. We've had a tumultuous relationship throughout the years due to his absence earlier in my life. I didn't understand how much our relationship affected me even after I believed I was healed.

For years, I would make the claim that I would be a better father than my own because he was not present, and I recognized that I will be a dope dad because I want to be a dope dad. ...not as a reaction to my relationship with my own father but as a choice. Once I let go of that yearning desire to be "better than," the pressure of what I believed a good dad to be started melting away. I know I'm going to make mistakes and won't always get it right, but the goal is to never give up. These Black dads helped me understand that it's going to be alright!

****

"You are doing just fine. There are no secrets to fatherhood. Just do your best." –J. Wimbley

"You are here. You are involved. You matter. You are critical. Whatever the opposition, remember you matter to this child and their quality of life." –K. Burrell

"Much like you challenge yourself to grow in your career and/or marriage, apply the same standard to how you parent. Nothing is off limits. Be comfortable being uncomfortable. Especially if you have girls. Ha!

Lastly, know that you create what you allow. That's the motto I live by in life and as a parent. Set the ground rules now to save yourself the pain and suffering later. We're all creatures of habit. Without structure, you'll never be able to assist your child in reaching their true potential. That being said, be sure to always mix structure with a lot of love. The child can digest it [discipline] so much better with the right seasoning. :) –D. Shannon

"Immerse yourself in the knowledge of God, which is the knowledge of self. Once you do that, you will have a proper understanding of your role in your new growing family. A weak spiritual relationship with your creator will create a weak relationship with your family because as the head of a family, balance is critical." –A. Arbyummi

"Raise them to be individuals with morals and values, and don't lie to them. Encourage them, and give them tough love as well. Respect your kids." –D. Davis

"Know that you're a Black father and it's an automatic target to be a Black father in the world. Nevertheless, stay strong!" –R. Bottoms

"Being a Black father is not for the faint of heart. It's a job in and of itself. Some step up to the plate and some do not. Make sure you are supporting the mother of your child at all times. They are carrying your child, and it's not easy... so continue to love them and pray for them. –R. Smith

"Don't listen to the master narrative regarding Black men. Consider that though they love you, your parents did not make all the right choices. You won't either. Show yourself grace. Lastly, they aren't coloring books you fill in with *your* colors. Let them become. It's hard when they end up dressing weird, but they eventually come home." –Dr. Yuille

"Take advantage of every opportunity. There are a lot of Black children in the world without parents. God willing, make sure your child does not become part of the statistic. Love your child." –X. Postell

"As a Black father, I take pride in showing my son how to be a Black man in America. In life, there are things we must teach our young sons and daughters that no one else can show them but us. Never let society, TV, or anyone else outside of your home teach your child anything before you do." –J. Martin

My goal with *Dear Black Dads: Wisdom for Your Journey to Fatherhood* is to provide Black dads a space to share insight and advice to support the next generations of leaders and change agents. This piece of literature is to resolve some of the fears that came with the utmost important role that any of us will ever carry: fatherhood. Imagine this book as a conversation with your friends...your fraternity brother...your bestie. As we all traverse this new land into fatherhood, it is important to me that we know as Black men, we are not alone. Some of us are well-versed in this role, whereas many of us are first timers who can't always turn to family due to past hurt or pain. Many of us are first timers who find it difficult to talk to our partners. Many of us are first timers who don't have a blueprint to show us how to serve in this role. And if you are *that* Black dad, I believe these words are a good start. This book was handcrafted especially for you!

After reading all of the responses from so many brothers, I feel more than prepared to address the challenges that come with fatherhood while supporting my wife the best I can. I feel affirmed in my ability to lead my family unit in a way that honors and respects them. The pressure to be a perfect father is no longer weighing down on my shoulders, and I can tell my head is held higher because of the wise words from the Black dads mentioned in this book.

JAMAL J. MYRICK

ACKNOWLEDGEMENTS

First and foremost, I want to thank God for providing this vision to touch the lives of other Black men throughout the world with intentionality and love. I was reminded by a friend from college how I spoke about creating this book almost 10-years ago. I'm happy that God created space for this wonderful labor of love.

Thank you to my grandfather, William P. Beasley, for providing me some of the earliest displays of Black fatherhood.

Thank you to my own father for being able to sit in the mess and grow together.

Thank you to each Black father who contributed to the book. Brothers, thank you for sharing your time and energy with the world in hopes of continuing to change the narratives of Black dads. I appreciate each of you for trusting my vision and allowing me to hold your words and stories high. Each of you kings are amazing!

Thank you to my editor, Nailah Harvey, for the support in this endeavor. You helped me more than you know.

Thank you to my blood brother, Dante Bonilla, for hearing my vent sessions and taking time to hear me out about this idea from start to finish.

Thank you to Tres Doctores for pushing me to keep reaching new heights!

Thank you to my dear fraternity brothers for the support and showing me excellent examples of fatherhood. *06!*

Thank you to the Black women who love, challenge, and fight the world with us. Special shout-out to my own wife! Tash, you've been a major support throughout this part of the journey and I'm thankful that we had our amazing phone conversation so many years ago. You're a phenomenal Black woman who's an amazing mother.

To my cohort member and brother, Dr. Luke Makwakwa, thank you. I wish we had the opportunity to connect once more before you went to your heavenly family. I've learned so much from you and I hope you know that your spirit will live on. Rest in power.

And finally, thank YOU, the reader for staying committed to reading this labor of love! I appreciate you. I hope you find a few nuggets of wisdom from these wonderful brothers who are trying their best to change the next generation of Black leaders.

ABOUT THE AUTHOR

Jamal J. Myrick, Ed.d.

Jamal J. Myrick, Ed.D. is a Black father, higher educator hustler, writer, reader, guest speaker, and lover of all things Black. He's a firm believer in living a life on purpose and strives to create positive change one connec-

tion at a time. When he's not loving up on his newborn and his wife, Dr. Myrick is traveling, in the community with his fraternity, or reading 2-3 good books. You can catch Dr. Myrick on melanatedandeducated.com or join his book club, blackvernacularbookclub.com. Email him at myrick.jamal@melanatedandeducated.com.

Made in the USA
Las Vegas, NV
20 April 2021

21740290R00031